AI Expense Tracking, Write-Offs & Depreciation

Optimizing Business Taxes with Artificial Intelligence

By Joe Correa

Published by Live Stronger Faster

This book is for educational and informational purposes only. The author and publisher are not engaged in rendering legal, financial, tax, or other professional advice. Readers should consult a qualified professional before making any financial decisions.

First Edition

Table of Contents

Introduction

In the modern business world, profits are no longer determined solely by how much revenue you generate, but by how much of that revenue you are allowed to keep, and this is where the real power of artificial intelligence begins to reveal itself, because most businesses do not lose money due to poor sales but because they silently overpay in taxes, miss deductions, misclassify expenses, and fail to apply depreciation correctly, which means they voluntarily hand over tens or hundreds of thousands of dollars every year simply because their financial systems cannot see what an intelligent algorithm can see, and this book exists to show you how AI now acts as a digital tax strategist that never sleeps, never forgets, and never misses a deductible dollar, scanning every transaction, every receipt, every bank feed, and every financial pattern inside your company to uncover hidden write-offs, maximize legal deductions, and apply depreciation with mathematical precision so that your business operates at peak tax efficiency year after year.

For decades, expense tracking was one of the most broken and dangerous areas of business finance, because it depended on humans manually entering data, categorizing purchases, attaching receipts, and remembering what qualified as a deduction, which inevitably meant that mistakes, oversights, and inconsistencies were built into the system, allowing tax dollars to leak out quietly through forgotten meals, miscategorized travel, unclaimed home-office deductions, improperly depreciated equipment, and inventory that was never written off, but with artificial intelligence now embedded inside accounting platforms, bank feeds, and expense management systems, every dollar that moves through your business becomes a data point that can be instantly classified, cross-checked against tax law, and optimized for deduction eligibility, turning what was once a chaotic paper-based process into a living, intelligent financial organism that continuously learns, improves, and protects your profit margins automatically.

AI changes the rules because it does not simply record what you spend, it understands what you spend it on, why you spent it, how it relates to your business activity, and how it should be treated under tax law, meaning that when you buy software, equipment, marketing, education, vehicles, real estate, or digital services, an AI-powered expense engine can immediately determine whether that cost should be expensed, capitalized, amortized, or depreciated, and it can apply the correct tax treatment in real time instead of leaving that decision to a rushed bookkeeper months later, which not only increases deductions but dramatically reduces audit risk because your records become internally consistent, logically defensible, and backed by data rather than guesswork.

One of the most powerful but misunderstood areas of tax savings is depreciation, and this is where AI becomes a true financial weapon for business owners, because depreciation is not just about spreading out the cost of assets over time but about strategically timing when and how those deductions are taken in order to minimize tax liability, manage cash flow, and align tax savings with growth plans, and when AI models analyze your balance sheet, income projections, asset purchases, and tax brackets, they can automatically select the most advantageous depreciation schedules, apply bonus depreciation or Section 179 where appropriate, and even simulate multiple scenarios so you can see how different write-off strategies affect your taxes years into the future, something that once required expensive CPAs and complex spreadsheets but now happens instantly inside modern AI-driven accounting systems.

What makes AI-powered expense and depreciation systems so revolutionary is that they do not operate in isolation, but connect directly to your bank accounts, credit cards, payroll, inventory systems, and accounting software, meaning that no transaction ever falls through the cracks, and every expense is automatically matched to receipts, vendor histories, and business purpose classifications, creating an audit-ready trail of proof that supports every deduction you claim, which means that instead of fearing an audit, your business becomes structurally resistant to one, because your records are not just complete but intelligently organized, cross-validated, and supported by machine-verified documentation that shows exactly how and why every dollar was deducted.

This book will show you how AI turns everyday spending into a profit-protection system, where routine business purchases such as travel, meals, advertising, software subscriptions, equipment, vehicles, and even your home office become part of a larger automated deduction engine that continuously works behind the scenes to lower your tax bill, because AI can detect patterns humans miss, such as when multiple small recurring charges add up to a large deductible expense, when personal and business spending overlap, when vendor behavior changes, or when asset usage qualifies for accelerated write-offs, allowing your business to legally capture more deductions without increasing risk, paperwork, or administrative burden.

As businesses grow more complex with remote teams, digital tools, e-commerce platforms, and multi-channel sales, traditional expense tracking breaks down even faster, because transactions flow through dozens of systems and currencies, making it almost impossible for humans to accurately track everything, but AI thrives in complexity, because it can process thousands of transactions per second, reconcile discrepancies, detect anomalies, and flag missing documentation automatically, which means your tax records stay clean, accurate, and optimized even as your company scales, expands internationally, or moves into new lines of business, ensuring that growth does not come with hidden tax inefficiencies.

Inside this book, you will learn how modern AI systems classify expenses, apply tax rules, manage depreciation, and continuously improve deduction accuracy over time, how machine learning models identify opportunities for write-offs that human accountants often miss, how automated receipt capture and bank feed integration eliminate documentation gaps, and how predictive algorithms forecast future deductions so you can plan major purchases at the most tax-advantageous times, giving you not just a historical record of what happened but a forward-looking strategy for how to legally minimize taxes before they are even owed.

This is not about aggressive tax schemes or risky loopholes, but about precision, consistency, and optimization, because AI does not guess or cut corners, it calculates, cross-references, and applies the law exactly as written, allowing businesses to claim everything they are legally entitled to without fear, delay, or error, and when your expense tracking and depreciation are handled by intelligent systems instead of memory and manual entry, your business shifts from being reactive at tax time to being proactive every single day, continuously building a stronger financial position with every transaction you make.

By the time you finish this introduction, you will understand that AI-powered expense tracking and depreciation is not a back-office tool but a profit engine, one that transforms ordinary business spending into a strategic advantage, one that shields your income, strengthens your balance sheet, and gives you the confidence to grow, invest, and expand knowing that your financial foundation is being protected by algorithms designed to see what humans cannot, calculate what humans would never have time to calculate, and apply the tax code with a level of accuracy and consistency that was impossible before artificial intelligence entered the world of business finance.

Chapter 1

The Hidden Power of AI Expense Intelligence

In the modern digital economy, every dollar that moves through a business leaves behind a trail of data, and for the first time in history artificial intelligence is able to read, understand, and interpret that data in ways that completely transform how companies manage expenses, deductions, and profitability, because instead of treating expenses as simple bookkeeping entries, AI now views them as dynamic financial signals that reveal how a business operates, grows, and protects itself from unnecessary taxation, which means that what was once a boring administrative function has become one of the most powerful profit-maximization tools available to business owners who understand how to use it correctly.

Traditional expense tracking was built for a paper world where receipts were stored in boxes and spreadsheets were updated manually, but AI-powered systems work in real time, connecting directly to bank accounts, credit cards, payroll systems, accounting platforms, and even vendor databases, allowing every transaction to be instantly captured, categorized, and evaluated against tax rules, industry benchmarks, and historical behavior, so instead of waiting until the end of the year to find out what happened to your money, you have a continuously updating financial map that shows exactly where every dollar went and how it can legally reduce your tax burden.

The true advantage of AI is that it does not simply record expenses, it understands them, because machine learning models are trained on millions of real-world transactions, tax codes, accounting standards, and audit patterns, which allows them to identify whether a purchase qualifies as advertising, education, equipment, travel, software, meals, or capital assets, and then apply the correct tax treatment automatically, eliminating the human errors that so often result in lost deductions, misclassified costs, or red flags that trigger audits.

This intelligent classification is what allows AI to unlock hidden write-offs, because many expenses that business owners assume are partially or fully non-deductible are actually eligible when properly documented and categorized, and AI systems are able to cross-check receipts, transaction descriptions, vendor histories, and business activities to build a legally defensible deduction profile that maximizes what can be claimed while maintaining full compliance with tax regulations.

AI also revolutionizes how businesses handle recurring expenses, which are one of the biggest sources of wasted money and missed deductions, because algorithms can detect patterns such as subscription creep, duplicate charges, underutilized software, and improperly categorized services, allowing businesses not only to write them off correctly but to eliminate unnecessary spending altogether, turning expense management into a continuous profit-optimization process instead of a once-a-year cleanup.

As your company grows, AI becomes even more valuable because complexity increases exponentially with every new product, employee, market, and platform, yet intelligent systems thrive in complexity, continuously reconciling data from multiple sources, flagging inconsistencies, and ensuring that your financial records remain clean, accurate, and audit-ready regardless of scale, which means you can expand confidently without creating tax chaos behind the scenes.

What this means for business owners is simple but profound: AI expense intelligence transforms spending into strategy, because every purchase becomes part of a larger automated system that protects cash flow, increases deductions, reduces risk, and builds long-term financial stability, turning your accounting infrastructure into one of the most powerful competitive advantages your company can possess.

The Ledger That Changed Everything

When Daniel Alvarez launched his digital marketing agency from a spare bedroom, he never imagined that something as simple as expense tracking would determine whether his business survived or collapsed, because in the early days money was coming in fast and going out even faster, and between ad costs, freelancers, software subscriptions, travel, and client entertainment, his bank account told one story while his spreadsheets told another, and neither of them ever matched what his accountant reported at tax time.

At first Daniel assumed that this confusion was just part of running a growing company, but as his revenue climbed past six figures he began to realize that he was paying far more in taxes than other agency owners he knew, even though their businesses were similar in size, and no matter how many receipts he gathered or how carefully he filled out spreadsheets, the numbers never seemed to work in his favor.

Everything changed the day a fellow entrepreneur introduced him to an AI-powered expense and deduction system that connected directly to his bank and credit cards, and within hours it began to map every transaction, recognize vendors, classify spending, and identify which costs were fully deductible, partially deductible, or miscategorized, and for the first time Daniel saw a clear, real-time picture of how his money was actually being used.

Within weeks the system uncovered thousands of dollars in missed write-offs from prior months, including software subscriptions, education expenses, home office deductions, and equipment purchases that had never been properly documented, and even more shocking was how the AI suggested new ways to structure upcoming purchases so they would qualify for accelerated deductions, legally reducing his tax burden before he even spent the money.

As the months passed, Daniel watched his cash flow improve even though his revenue stayed the same, because the AI was quietly working behind the scenes to ensure that every dollar he spent was being treated in the most tax-efficient way possible, turning ordinary business operations into a constant stream of financial optimization that no human bookkeeper could have matched.

By the end of the year, when his accountant reviewed the AI-generated financial records, there were no missing receipts, no unexplained numbers, and no confusion about what qualified as a deduction, and for the first time Daniel filed a return that felt not just accurate but strategically designed to protect his business and his future. Looking back, Daniel realized that the true breakthrough was not just saving money on taxes, but gaining control over his finances, because with AI managing his expenses, deductions, and documentation, he no longer feared growth, audits, or complexity, knowing that every transaction was being watched, optimized, and transformed into long-term profit by an intelligent system that never missed a thing.

Chapter 2

How AI Finds Deductions Humans Never See

In every business, thousands of small financial decisions are made every year, from buying software to paying contractors, from advertising to travel, and while each expense may seem insignificant on its own, together they form the hidden architecture of a company's tax position, yet most of these transactions are processed by humans who simply do not have the time, memory, or analytical capacity to evaluate every purchase against the full complexity of tax law, which is why artificial intelligence now plays such a critical role, because it can instantly scan, cross-reference, and analyze every transaction in ways no human team ever could, turning ordinary spending into a continuous deduction discovery engine that quietly finds money the business would otherwise lose.

AI is able to detect deductible patterns because it is trained on vast libraries of tax codes, court rulings, accounting standards, and historical audit outcomes, allowing it to understand not just what an expense is, but how similar expenses have been treated in thousands of real-world tax filings, which means when your business pays for cloud software, professional education, home office equipment, internet service, digital advertising, or even business meals, the AI can immediately determine how that cost should be classified, what percentage is deductible, and whether it should be expensed immediately or depreciated over time, eliminating the guesswork that so often leaves deductions unclaimed.

One of the most powerful ways AI finds hidden deductions is by recognizing relationships between expenses that humans tend to see as separate, because while a bookkeeper may categorize your laptop, your software subscriptions, and your online training as three different line items, an AI system understands that they are all part of a single business function, such as digital operations or professional development, allowing it to build a stronger and more defensible deduction profile that maximizes what can be written off without increasing risk.

AI also excels at uncovering partial deductions that most businesses ignore, such as mixed-use expenses for vehicles, phones, internet, home offices, and even meals, because instead of forcing you to choose between business and personal use, intelligent systems can analyze usage patterns, locations, time stamps, and historical behavior to determine what portion of each expense is legitimately tied to business activity, which means you are no longer leaving money on the table simply because it was too complicated to calculate manually.

Another area where AI outperforms traditional accounting is in its ability to continuously update deduction strategies as tax laws change, because machine learning models are constantly trained on new regulations, IRS guidance, and legal precedents, ensuring that your expense classifications remain current, compliant, and optimized, so instead of relying on last year's rules, your business operates under the most up-to-date interpretation of the tax code every single day.

What truly makes AI revolutionary is that it does not wait until tax season to start looking for deductions, but instead operates in real time, analyzing transactions as they occur and providing immediate feedback on how purchases should be structured, documented, or timed to maximize tax benefits, which means that instead of reacting to your tax bill after it arrives, you are proactively shaping it throughout the year with every financial decision you make.

This transforms the role of expense tracking from passive record-keeping into active tax strategy, because AI does not simply ask what happened, it asks what could have happened, what should happen next, and how future spending can be aligned with deduction opportunities, allowing businesses to turn everyday operations into a powerful, automated tax-optimization engine that continuously works to protect profits and strengthen financial stability.

The Invisible Money Trail

When Maya Chen opened her e-commerce brand selling wellness products online, she focused all her energy on marketing, inventory, and customer experience, never realizing that thousands of dollars were quietly slipping away through missed deductions, because her accounting system treated every expense as just another line item instead of part of a larger financial story waiting to be told.

It was not until she began using an AI-powered expense platform that she saw what had been hiding in plain sight, as the software began grouping her advertising costs, website subscriptions, design tools, shipping software, and professional coaching into interconnected categories that revealed how deeply her business depended on digital infrastructure, unlocking deductions that had never been properly claimed before.

Within weeks, the AI identified that a large portion of her home internet, phone usage, and even her living space qualified for business deductions because of how her company actually operated, and by analyzing time logs, sales activity, and order fulfillment patterns, it was able to assign precise percentages to each mixed-use expense, turning what once seemed like personal costs into legally defensible business write-offs.

The real shock came when the system reviewed her prior-year data and uncovered thousands of dollars in overpaid taxes due to expenses that had been misclassified or ignored, and for the first time Maya realized that her business had not been unprofitable, it had simply been poorly optimized from a tax perspective.

As the months passed, Maya began making smarter purchasing decisions, guided by the AI's real-time feedback, timing equipment upgrades, software renewals, and marketing campaigns to align with the most advantageous deduction windows, effectively reshaping her financial future without changing a single thing about her core business model.

By the end of the year, her tax bill was dramatically lower, her records were perfectly organized, and her confidence as a business owner had grown, because she finally understood that success was not just about how much she sold, but about how intelligently her expenses were structured and protected.

Looking back, Maya realized that the true value of AI was not just in finding hidden money, but in revealing the invisible patterns that governed her entire business, allowing her to follow the trail of deductions that had always been there, waiting for a machine intelligent enough to see them.

Chapter 3

Mastering Depreciation With AI Precision

Depreciation has always been one of the most powerful but misunderstood tools in the tax code, because it allows businesses to transform large capital purchases into long-term tax shields, yet most companies either apply it incorrectly or fail to use it strategically, which is where artificial intelligence changes everything by bringing mathematical precision, forecasting intelligence, and automated compliance into what was once a confusing, error-prone accounting process that quietly cost business owners enormous amounts of money every year.

At its core, depreciation is about matching the cost of an asset to the income it helps generate, but the tax code provides multiple methods for doing this, including straight-line depreciation, accelerated methods, bonus depreciation, and Section 179 expensing, and each one can dramatically change how much tax you pay and when you pay it, yet choosing the right method requires analyzing cash flow, growth plans, tax brackets, and future income, which is far beyond what most small business accounting systems were ever designed to do, but AI models are built precisely for this kind of multi-variable financial optimization.

When an AI-powered system sees your business purchase equipment, vehicles, computers, machinery, or even digital infrastructure, it does not simply log the cost, but immediately evaluates how that asset will be used, how long it will generate value, what tax brackets your business is in now and in the future, and how different depreciation schedules will affect your tax burden over time, allowing it to automatically select the method that produces the greatest legal tax advantage while maintaining full compliance with tax regulations.

This is especially powerful for growing businesses, because timing matters just as much as totals, and AI can simulate how accelerating depreciation in one year might free up cash for expansion, while spreading it out in another year might reduce tax volatility, giving business owners the ability to use depreciation not just as a reporting tool but as a strategic lever that supports long-term growth, stability, and reinvestment.

AI also eliminates one of the biggest risks in depreciation, which is inconsistency, because when assets are tracked manually, it is common for items to be forgotten, double-counted, or misclassified, leading to discrepancies that raise audit risk and reduce deduction accuracy, but intelligent systems maintain a continuously updated asset ledger that tracks purchase dates, costs, usage, improvements, disposals, and depreciation schedules automatically, creating a single source of truth that ensures every asset is accounted for and optimized.

Another advantage of AI-driven depreciation is its ability to handle complex scenarios, such as partial business use, upgrades, repairs, and asset disposals, because instead of forcing accountants to manually adjust schedules, machine learning models can recalculate depreciation in real time, ensuring that tax benefits remain accurate and defensible even as assets are repurposed, sold, or modified, which is especially valuable for businesses that rely on technology, vehicles, or rapidly evolving equipment.

Ultimately, AI transforms depreciation from a backward-looking accounting exercise into a forward-looking financial strategy, because by continuously forecasting income, expenses, and tax exposure, intelligent systems allow businesses to plan asset purchases with precision, knowing exactly how each investment will affect taxes, cash flow, and profitability for years to come, turning what was once a confusing tax rule into one of the most powerful tools for building long-term financial strength.

The Assets That Paid for Themselves

When Carlos Rivera expanded his construction company, he invested heavily in trucks, heavy equipment, and digital project management tools, believing that growth required upfront spending, but when tax season arrived, he was shocked by how little of that investment seemed to translate into tax relief, leaving him wondering whether the risk he had taken was truly worth it.

It was only after he adopted an AI-powered accounting and depreciation system that the real value of his assets began to reveal itself, as the software analyzed each purchase, evaluated how it was used in the business, and automatically applied the most advantageous depreciation methods, turning what had once been simple expenses into powerful tax shields that reduced his liability year after year.

The AI even suggested adjusting the timing of future equipment purchases to align with projected revenue spikes, allowing Carlos to strategically accelerate or spread out deductions depending on his cash flow needs, which gave him a level of financial control he had never experienced before.

When one of his trucks was sold and replaced, the system automatically recalculated the remaining depreciation, captured the appropriate gains or losses, and updated his financial forecasts, eliminating the confusion and errors that had plagued his previous manual accounting process.

By the end of the second year, Carlos realized that his equipment was no longer just a cost of doing business, but a carefully managed portfolio of tax-optimized assets that effectively paid for themselves through reduced tax bills and improved cash flow.

His accountant was amazed at how clean, consistent, and audit-ready the records had become, because every asset was tracked, every schedule was justified, and every deduction was supported by data, making the company both more profitable and less risky at the same time.

Looking back, Carlos understood that the true power of AI was not just in automating depreciation, but in transforming how he viewed investment itself, because every truck, machine, and tool was now part of a larger financial strategy designed to build wealth, not just get the job done.

Chapter 4

Real-Time Expense Automation and Continuous Tax Optimization

The most profound shift artificial intelligence brings to business finance is not simply better recordkeeping, but the move from static, after-the-fact accounting to real-time expense automation that continuously optimizes a company's tax position as money flows in and out, because when expenses are captured, analyzed, and classified the moment they occur, tax efficiency stops being a seasonal event and becomes a living system that operates every single day the business is open.

Traditional accounting systems were designed for monthly or quarterly review cycles, meaning expenses were recorded long after decisions were made, often when receipts were missing, memories had faded, and opportunities for strategic adjustments were already gone, but AI-driven expense automation reverses this entire model by integrating directly with bank feeds, payment processors, expense apps, invoicing platforms, and accounting software, ensuring that every transaction is instantly recorded, categorized, and evaluated for tax treatment before it ever becomes a problem. This real-time visibility changes behavior at the operational level, because when business owners and managers see how each purchase affects deductions, cash flow, and tax exposure immediately, financial decisions become smarter by default, as AI systems provide contextual guidance, flagging when expenses may require additional documentation, suggesting alternative classifications, or warning when spending patterns drift away from optimal tax efficiency.

One of the most powerful outcomes of continuous expense automation is consistency, because AI applies the same logic, rules, and classification standards to every transaction, eliminating the variability that occurs when multiple people manually code expenses differently, which not only increases deduction accuracy but also creates clean, defensible records that dramatically reduce audit risk and compliance stress.

AI systems also excel at detecting anomalies in real time, such as unusual vendor charges, duplicate expenses, missing receipts, or sudden changes in spending behavior, allowing businesses to correct issues immediately instead of discovering them months later during reconciliation or audits, transforming expense management from a reactive cleanup process into proactive financial control.

As expenses are continuously optimized, AI also builds predictive models that forecast future deductions, cash flow, and tax liability based on current spending patterns, enabling businesses to plan purchases, expansions, and investments with precision, knowing how each decision will impact taxes long before filings are due, which turns expense management into a strategic planning tool rather than a compliance burden.

Ultimately, real-time expense automation allows businesses to operate in a state of permanent tax readiness, where records are always complete, deductions are always optimized, and financial decisions are always informed by intelligent systems, creating a foundation of stability and efficiency that allows companies to scale confidently without losing control of their tax position.

The Business That Never Waited for Tax Season

When Olivia Martinez scaled her remote consulting firm from a solo practice into a multi-six-figure operation, she expected complexity, but she did not expect the constant anxiety that came from never knowing where her finances truly stood, because expenses flowed through dozens of tools, subscriptions, contractors, and platforms, leaving her unsure whether she was optimized or exposed.

After adopting an AI-powered real-time expense automation system, Olivia watched as her financial world reorganized itself almost overnight, with transactions appearing instantly, expenses categorized automatically, and deductions identified in real time, giving her a clarity she had never experienced before.

The system flagged missing receipts the same day purchases were made, suggested documentation improvements, and even warned her when spending patterns might reduce deduction eligibility, allowing her to make small adjustments that compounded into massive savings over time.

As the year progressed, Olivia stopped fearing tax season entirely, because she no longer had to scramble to reconstruct financial history, knowing instead that her records were always complete, accurate, and optimized, no matter how fast her business grew.

When her accountant reviewed the year-end reports, they found no inconsistencies, no surprises, and no missed opportunities, because every decision had already been evaluated and optimized by AI long before the return was prepared.

What surprised Olivia most was not just the money saved, but the peace of mind gained, because for the first time her business felt financially self-aware, capable of adjusting itself continuously without waiting for human intervention.

Looking back, she realized that the real breakthrough was not automation alone, but the freedom that came from knowing her business was always ready, always optimized, and never waiting for tax season to take control again.

Chapter 5

Audit-Proof Expense Systems and AI-Driven Compliance

For most business owners, the fear of an audit is not rooted in wrongdoing but in uncertainty, because traditional expense tracking systems are fragmented, inconsistent, and heavily dependent on human memory, making it difficult to prove why expenses were deducted, how they were classified, and whether documentation truly supports the tax positions taken, yet artificial intelligence fundamentally reshapes this reality by transforming expense management into an always-on compliance system that continuously builds audit-ready records without adding friction or fear to daily operations.

At the heart of audit risk is inconsistency, because auditors are not only looking for incorrect deductions but for patterns that suggest careless or unreliable recordkeeping, such as mismatched categories, missing receipts, unexplained fluctuations, or expenses that do not clearly align with business activity, and AI addresses this problem directly by applying uniform logic to every transaction, ensuring that similar expenses are treated the same way every time, creating a clean, repeatable, and defensible financial narrative that holds up under scrutiny.

AI-powered expense systems automatically link each transaction to supporting evidence, including digital receipts, vendor histories, timestamps, geolocation data, and usage context, meaning that every deduction is backed by a structured data trail rather than a loose collection of files, which allows businesses to instantly produce proof when required instead of scrambling to reconstruct records months or years later, dramatically reducing both audit exposure and stress.

Another major advantage of AI is its ability to continuously cross-check expenses against compliance rules, because tax regulations are not static and vary by jurisdiction, expense type, and business structure, yet machine learning models are designed to ingest regulatory updates, IRS guidance, and enforcement trends, allowing expense classifications to remain current and compliant without requiring business owners to manually track every change in the law.

AI also plays a critical role in detecting internal risks before they become external problems, because intelligent systems can flag anomalies such as unusually high deductions in specific categories, sudden shifts in spending behavior, or expenses that fall outside normal business patterns, giving companies the opportunity to review, correct, or document transactions proactively rather than explaining them reactively during an audit.

As businesses scale, the compliance burden grows exponentially, especially when teams expand, remote work increases, and spending authority is distributed across employees and contractors, but AI-driven expense governance allows companies to enforce rules automatically, applying spending policies, approval workflows, and documentation requirements consistently across the organization, ensuring that compliance is built into the system rather than enforced manually after the fact.

By turning expense tracking into a continuous compliance engine, AI eliminates the traditional tradeoff between maximizing deductions and minimizing risk, because businesses no longer have to choose between claiming what they are entitled to and staying audit-safe, as intelligent systems make it possible to do both simultaneously, creating a financial environment where confidence replaces fear and compliance becomes a natural byproduct of intelligent automation.

The Audit That Never Happened

When Marcus Bennett received a notice from the tax authorities requesting additional information about his consulting firm's deductions, his initial reaction was panic, because despite running an honest business, he knew his expense records were scattered across emails, spreadsheets, and old folders, leaving him unsure whether he could defend every decision made over the past several years.

What Marcus did not realize was that months earlier he had implemented an AI-powered expense and compliance system that had been quietly organizing his financial life, linking every transaction to receipts, vendor profiles, and business purposes, and applying consistent classification logic without requiring his attention.

As he logged into the system, he was stunned to see that every questioned expense already had a complete audit trail, including timestamps, categorization logic, and documentation explaining exactly how the deduction aligned with business activity, allowing him to respond to the inquiry calmly and confidently.

The AI even highlighted potential areas of concern in advance, suggesting additional notes and supporting context that strengthened his position before any human ever reviewed the file, transforming what could have been a stressful ordeal into a straightforward administrative task.

Days later, Marcus received confirmation that no further

action was required, and the audit request was closed without escalation, leaving him with a profound realization that the system had not merely saved him time, but had protected his business at a structural level.

In the months that followed, Marcus stopped worrying about audits entirely, knowing that his expense system was continuously enforcing compliance, consistency, and documentation, regardless of how busy or complex his operations became.

Looking back, he understood that the true value of AI was not in reacting to audits, but in making them unnecessary, because when every expense is recorded, justified, and optimized in real time, there is nothing left to fear, only proof waiting quietly in the background.

Chapter 6

Turning Everyday Spending Into a Long-Term Tax Advantage

Most businesses think of expenses as something to control or reduce, but artificial intelligence reframes expenses as something to **design**, because when spending is tracked, classified, and optimized intelligently, it becomes one of the most powerful long-term tax and profit strategies a business can deploy, allowing ordinary operational costs to compound into sustained financial advantages that grow stronger with time instead of disappearing at the end of each tax year.

The key difference between traditional expense management and AI-driven expense intelligence is intentionality, because manual systems merely record what happened, while AI systems continuously analyze how spending decisions interact with tax rules, cash flow cycles, depreciation schedules, and future growth plans, meaning that each dollar spent is evaluated not just for necessity but for strategic impact, turning routine purchases into deliberate financial moves that strengthen the business over multiple years.

AI excels at identifying spending behaviors that quietly create tax inefficiencies, such as poorly timed purchases, misaligned subscription renewals, inconsistent categorization, or asset acquisitions that fail to maximize depreciation benefits, and by correcting these patterns early, businesses avoid compounding losses that would otherwise persist year after year, replacing them with optimized structures that improve tax efficiency automatically as the company grows.

One of the most powerful long-term advantages AI creates is continuity, because intelligent systems maintain consistent treatment of expenses across tax years, ensuring that deductions, depreciation schedules, and documentation remain aligned over time, which is critical for avoiding red flags, supporting future audits, and preserving tax benefits that span multiple reporting periods, especially for assets, software, and infrastructure that generate value long after their purchase date.

AI also enables businesses to strategically plan spending cycles around tax outcomes, because by forecasting revenue, profit margins, and tax exposure, intelligent systems can recommend when to accelerate expenses, when to defer purchases, and when to invest in assets that create long-term deductions, allowing business owners to smooth tax liability, protect cash flow, and avoid sudden financial shocks that often occur when tax planning is reactive instead of proactive. As businesses scale, AI becomes even more valuable because the volume of transactions increases dramatically, and without intelligent systems, small inefficiencies multiply into massive financial leakage, yet AI thrives on scale, using larger datasets to refine predictions, improve categorization accuracy, and uncover new deduction opportunities that only emerge when spending reaches a certain level of complexity, turning growth itself into a source of tax intelligence rather than risk.

Ultimately, AI transforms expense management into a compounding system, where every transaction strengthens the financial foundation of the business, every tax year builds on the last, and every decision contributes to a long-term strategy designed to minimize taxes legally, stabilize cash flow, and maximize retained earnings, allowing companies to operate with confidence, foresight, and financial discipline that was once reserved only for large corporations with elite advisory teams.

Seven Years of Invisible Wins

When Aaron Whitfield started his software consulting firm, he measured success the same way most entrepreneurs do, by monthly revenue, client count, and growth rate, never considering that the most important factor in his long-term wealth would be something far quieter and far less visible: how intelligently his business expenses were structured from the very beginning.

In the early years, Aaron tracked expenses manually, believing that good intentions and basic bookkeeping were enough, but despite steady growth, his profits never seemed to match the effort he put in, because each year his tax bill arrived like an unavoidable surprise, draining cash he could have reinvested into his company or saved for future opportunities.

Everything changed when he adopted an AI-driven expense intelligence system that did more than track spending, because it analyzed his entire financial history, mapped how his business actually operated, and began quietly restructuring how expenses were categorized, timed, and documented, not by changing what he bought, but by changing how those purchases were treated over time.

In the first year alone, the system uncovered inefficiencies that had gone unnoticed for years, such as software subscriptions that should have been grouped and depreciated differently, equipment purchases that could have generated larger deductions if timed correctly, and recurring expenses that were inconsistently classified, all of which were corrected automatically going forward, setting the foundation for compounding benefits.

As the years passed, Aaron noticed something subtle but powerful happening, because while his revenue grew steadily, his tax burden grew much more slowly, and in some years barely increased at all, even as the company expanded, because the AI continuously optimized depreciation schedules, aligned spending with projected income, and ensured that every legitimate deduction was captured with precision and consistency.

By year four, the system had built a multi-year financial narrative that told a clear, defensible story of growth, investment, and optimization, making audits a non-event and giving Aaron unprecedented confidence in his numbers, because he no longer wondered whether he had missed something, knowing that the system evaluated every transaction with more discipline and foresight than any human ever could.

What surprised him most was not just the tax savings, but the freedom it created, because with predictable cash flow and stable tax exposure, Aaron began making bolder strategic decisions, investing in new products, hiring talent, and expanding internationally, knowing that his financial infrastructure could support growth without collapsing under complexity.

By year six, the AI had become more than a tool, it had become an invisible partner, quietly learning from years of data, refining strategies, and anticipating future needs, ensuring that spending decisions made today would still be working in Aaron's favor years down the line, long after the original purchase receipts had faded from memory.

In the seventh year, when Aaron sold a minority stake in his company, the clean, consistent, AI-optimized financial records significantly increased the company's valuation, because investors saw not just revenue, but disciplined financial management, predictable tax exposure, and long-term efficiency baked into the business model.

Looking back, Aaron realized that the greatest wins had never been dramatic or visible, because they happened quietly, transaction by transaction, year by year, as AI transformed everyday spending into a series of invisible advantages that compounded over time, proving that true financial intelligence is not about chasing shortcuts, but about building systems that work tirelessly in your favor long after you stop thinking about them.

Chapter 7

Designing a Self-Optimizing Expense and Deduction Ecosystem

At a certain stage of growth, businesses discover that optimizing expenses one transaction at a time is no longer enough, because real financial power does not come from isolated deductions but from systems that continuously adapt, learn, and improve without requiring constant human oversight, and this is where artificial intelligence evolves from a helpful tool into a self-optimizing financial ecosystem that designs, maintains, and strengthens a company's tax position year after year.

A self-optimizing expense ecosystem begins with integration, because AI systems do not operate in silos but connect across banking, accounting, payroll, invoicing, procurement, asset management, and forecasting platforms, allowing financial intelligence to flow freely across the entire organization, which means every decision made in one area automatically informs optimization in another, eliminating blind spots that traditionally cause missed deductions and compliance gaps.

Once integrated, AI systems establish behavioral baselines by analyzing historical spending, revenue cycles, asset usage, and deduction patterns, creating a financial fingerprint unique to the business, and this baseline becomes the foundation for continuous improvement, because every new transaction is compared against what is normal, expected, and optimal, allowing the system to detect inefficiencies, opportunities, and risks the moment they emerge.

This ecosystem approach allows AI to move beyond categorization and into orchestration, because instead of simply asking where an expense belongs, intelligent systems ask how that expense fits into a broader strategy, whether it should be accelerated, deferred, bundled, depreciated, or restructured, and how it interacts with cash flow, growth objectives, and long-term tax exposure, effectively turning expense management into a form of automated financial design.

One of the most powerful features of a self-optimizing system is feedback, because AI continuously measures outcomes, comparing projected tax benefits to actual results, learning which strategies produce the best balance of savings, compliance, and flexibility, and then refining its recommendations accordingly, ensuring that the system becomes smarter over time rather than stagnating like static accounting rules.

As regulations evolve and tax laws change, AI ecosystems adapt automatically, ingesting new guidance, enforcement trends, and compliance thresholds, updating classification logic and deduction strategies without disrupting operations, which allows businesses to remain compliant without sacrificing optimization, even as complexity increases across jurisdictions, asset types, and business models.

Ultimately, a self-optimizing expense and deduction ecosystem creates a shift in mindset, because tax efficiency is no longer something businesses chase after the fact, but something embedded into every financial decision by design, creating a resilient, intelligent structure that protects profits, supports growth, and compounds advantages year after year with minimal friction and maximum precision.

The Company That Learned How to Think About Money

When Evelyn Brooks founded her logistics technology company, she built it with speed in mind, focusing relentlessly on innovation, customer acquisition, and scaling infrastructure, never pausing to question whether her financial systems were evolving at the same pace as the business itself.

In the early years, growth masked inefficiency, because rising revenue covered the quiet leaks caused by inconsistent expense tracking, fragmented systems, and reactive tax planning, but as the company crossed into eight-figure territory, those leaks became impossible to ignore, manifesting as volatile tax bills, unpredictable cash flow, and increasing compliance stress that threatened to slow momentum.

The turning point came when Evelyn authorized the deployment of a fully integrated AI-driven expense and deduction ecosystem, not as a single software upgrade, but as a structural redesign of how the company understood and managed money, connecting banking, accounting, procurement, payroll, asset tracking, and forecasting into one intelligent financial nervous system.

In the first year, the system focused on observation, quietly learning the rhythms of the business, mapping spending behavior, identifying recurring inefficiencies, and building a baseline model of how expenses interacted with revenue cycles, asset utilization, and tax exposure, producing insights that human teams had never had time or data to uncover.

By the second year, the AI began actively reshaping financial behavior, recommending changes in purchasing timing, restructuring subscription agreements, optimizing depreciation schedules, and aligning capital investments with projected revenue growth, all while maintaining perfect documentation and compliance, creating noticeable improvements in both cash flow stability and tax efficiency. What surprised Evelyn most was how the system improved decision-making across the organization, because department heads received real-time feedback on how spending choices affected long-term financial outcomes, gradually shifting the company culture from reactive budgeting to intentional financial design, where every expense was understood as part of a larger strategy.

In the third and fourth years, the ecosystem matured, continuously refining its models based on actual outcomes, learning which strategies produced the strongest results, and adjusting automatically as regulations evolved and the company expanded into new markets, ensuring that optimization kept pace with growth instead of lagging behind it.

By year five, audits became procedural rather than stressful, because every expense, asset, and deduction was supported by a consistent, machine-verified narrative that demonstrated discipline, intent, and compliance, reducing regulatory friction and increasing confidence among stakeholders and investors alike.

The most profound change came in year six, when Evelyn realized that financial uncertainty had disappeared entirely replaced by predictability and control, because the system could forecast tax exposure years in advance, simulate growth scenarios, and adapt spending strategies accordingly, allowing leadership to plan boldly without fear of financial surprises. In the seventh year, as acquisition offers began arriving, the company's valuation reflected not just its technology and market position, but the strength of its financial architecture, because buyers saw a business that did not merely track money, but understood it, optimized it, and learned from it continuously.

Looking back, Evelyn understood that the greatest achievement was not higher profits alone, but building a company that had learned how to think about money intelligently, because once financial intelligence became embedded into the system itself, growth no longer created chaos, but clarity, turning complexity into an asset rather than a liability.

Chapter 8

Scaling Without Losing Control: AI, Complexity, and Financial Discipline

As businesses scale, complexity does not increase linearly, it multiplies, because every new employee, vendor, market, product line, software tool, and jurisdiction adds layers of financial activity that interact in unpredictable ways, and it is precisely at this stage that many otherwise successful companies lose control of their expenses, deductions, and tax position, not because they are careless, but because their systems were never designed to operate intelligently at scale, which is why artificial intelligence becomes essential, not optional, for sustaining growth without sacrificing financial discipline.

In small businesses, expense decisions are usually centralized and visible, but as organizations grow, spending authority becomes distributed across departments, teams, contractors, and automated systems, creating fragmentation that traditional accounting cannot reconcile efficiently, yet AI thrives in distributed environments, because it can ingest data from countless sources simultaneously, normalize it, and apply consistent classification, compliance, and optimization logic across the entire organization, ensuring that growth does not dilute financial integrity.

AI-driven financial systems are uniquely suited to scaling environments because they are designed to learn patterns rather than enforce static rules, meaning they adapt as spending behavior evolves, new vendors appear, and operational models change, continuously refining how expenses are categorized, documented, and optimized so that accuracy improves with scale instead of deteriorating, which is the opposite of what happens in manual or spreadsheet-based systems.

One of the greatest dangers of rapid growth is the silent accumulation of inefficiencies, such as redundant subscriptions, misaligned procurement cycles, inconsistent expense policies, and underutilized assets, all of which quietly erode margins and inflate tax liability, yet AI detects these inefficiencies early by monitoring anomalies, trend deviations, and usage mismatches in real time, allowing businesses to correct course before losses compound over multiple years.

As companies expand across states, countries, or digital marketplaces, compliance becomes exponentially more complex, because tax treatment, documentation requirements, and reporting standards vary by jurisdiction, but AI systems are built to manage rule-based variation at scale, automatically applying the correct tax logic to each transaction based on location, entity structure, and regulatory context, ensuring that expansion does not create hidden compliance exposure or missed deductions.

AI also plays a critical role in maintaining strategic alignment during growth, because it connects expense behavior to long-term objectives, forecasting how today's spending decisions affect future tax exposure, cash flow, and profitability, allowing leadership to scale intentionally rather than reactively, with clear visibility into how complexity impacts financial outcomes.

Ultimately, AI allows businesses to scale without losing control because it replaces human limitation with machine consistency, foresight, and adaptability, transforming complexity from a liability into a structured system that supports sustainable growth, disciplined spending, and long-term tax optimization, even as the organization becomes larger, faster, and more globally interconnected.

The Weight of Growth

When Jonathan Hale launched his SaaS company, growth felt effortless, because each new customer validated the product, each new hire expanded capability, and each new market represented opportunity, but as revenue accelerated and operations spread across regions, Jonathan began to feel a growing unease that had nothing to do with sales and everything to do with money he could no longer clearly see.

At first, the signs were subtle, small discrepancies between departmental budgets and accounting reports, delayed reconciliations, rising tax estimates that seemed disproportionate to profit growth, and a growing sense that financial clarity was slipping just as the company was becoming truly successful.

Jonathan reassured himself that this was normal, that complexity was simply the cost of scale, but the discomfort deepened when an end-of-year tax projection revealed a liability far higher than expected, forcing the company to delay strategic investments and exposing how fragile their financial infrastructure had become beneath the surface of impressive growth metrics.

The decision to rebuild the company's financial systems around AI did not come easily, because it required confronting the reality that traditional tools and manual processes were no longer sufficient, but once implemented, the AI began by observing rather than intervening, mapping how money flowed through the organization, how expenses accumulated, and where inefficiencies quietly hid. Within months, the system revealed patterns no human team had fully grasped overlapping software licenses across departments, inconsistent expense categorization that inflated taxable income, procurement timing that increased tax exposure, and regional compliance mismatches that created unnecessary risk, all of which had grown organically alongside the company.

As the AI began making recommendations, Jonathan noticed a shift, not just in the numbers, but in organizational behavior, because managers received real-time insight into how spending decisions affected long-term financial outcomes, encouraging discipline without stifling innovation, and gradually replacing guesswork with informed intent.

Over the next year, the company continued to grow, but this time growth felt lighter, because complexity no longer translated into chaos, as expenses were optimized automatically, deductions were captured consistently, and compliance adapted seamlessly across jurisdictions, allowing leadership to focus on strategy instead of damage control.

What surprised Jonathan most was how the system improved forecasting accuracy, because for the first time, the company could project tax exposure and cash flow years ahead with confidence, making expansion decisions from a position of control rather than optimism alone. By the third year after implementation, audits became routine, investor confidence increased, and the company's valuation reflected not just revenue and technology, but operational maturity, because buyers and partners saw a business capable of scaling indefinitely without losing financial discipline.

Looking back, Jonathan realized that growth itself had never been the problem, because the true weight came from unmanaged complexity, and once AI absorbed that weight, transforming it into structured intelligence, growth no longer felt heavy, but balanced, sustainable, and fully within control.

Chapter 9

From Reactive Accounting to Predictive Tax Intelligence

For most of business history, accounting has been reactive by design, focused on recording what already happened, correcting mistakes after they occurred, and calculating tax liability once it was unavoidable, but artificial intelligence fundamentally changes this model by transforming expense tracking, deductions, and depreciation into a predictive intelligence system that allows businesses to anticipate tax outcomes long before they materialize, replacing surprise with foresight and uncertainty with strategic control.

Reactive accounting forces businesses into a defensive posture, because decisions are made first and explained later, often months after the fact, when there is little opportunity to adjust timing, structure, or documentation, yet AI-powered financial systems operate continuously, analyzing transaction data in real time and projecting how current behavior will influence future tax exposure, cash flow, and profitability, enabling companies to shape outcomes proactively instead of reacting to them under pressure. Predictive tax intelligence works by combining historical financial data, real-time expense activity, revenue forecasts, asset schedules, and current tax rules into forward-looking models that simulate multiple scenarios, allowing businesses to see how different spending patterns, investment decisions, or growth trajectories will affect their tax position across months and years, which elevates expense management from bookkeeping to strategic planning.

One of the most powerful benefits of predictive intelligence is timing optimization, because AI can identify when accelerating deductions will reduce near-term tax strain, when deferring expenses may smooth future liabilities, and when capital investments should be structured to maximize depreciation benefits based on projected income levels, allowing businesses to align financial decisions with long-term objectives rather than short-term convenience.

AI also improves resilience by identifying risk before it becomes visible to humans, because predictive models can flag when deduction ratios deviate from historical norms, when expense growth outpaces revenue in ways that could trigger scrutiny, or when compliance thresholds are approaching across jurisdictions, giving businesses time to adjust behavior and documentation proactively instead of responding defensively after an issue arises.

As predictive systems mature, they become increasingly personalized, learning the unique rhythms of a business, its seasonality, growth cycles, and operational dependencies, allowing tax strategies to evolve dynamically as the company changes, ensuring that optimization remains aligned with reality rather than static assumptions frozen in last year's spreadsheet.

Ultimately, predictive tax intelligence represents the final evolution of AI-driven expense and deduction systems, because it allows businesses not only to capture every legal deduction and maintain perfect compliance, but to plan confidently, invest strategically, and grow deliberately, knowing that future tax outcomes are no longer unknown variables but modeled, measured, and actively managed components of long-term success.

Seeing the Year Before It Happened

When Priya Nandakumar took over as CFO of a rapidly expanding professional services firm, she inherited impressive growth numbers alongside a persistent problem: every year ended with financial surprises that forced last-minute decisions, emergency cash reallocations, and uncomfortable conversations with leadership about why tax outcomes never matched expectations.

Despite having capable accountants and modern software, the company remained trapped in a reactive cycle, where expenses were tracked after the fact, deductions were discovered late, and tax planning amounted to educated guesses rather than informed strategy, leaving Priya frustrated by how little control the organization truly had over its financial future.

Her mandate was clear, eliminate surprises, and after months of evaluation, she led the implementation of an AI-driven predictive tax intelligence system designed not merely to record transactions, but to continuously model future outcomes based on real-time data, historical patterns, and regulatory context.

In the first months, the system focused on learning, absorbing years of financial history, identifying seasonal trends, mapping expense behavior to revenue cycles, and building a baseline forecast that revealed why prior tax surprises had been so consistent, exposing timing mismatches, poorly aligned depreciation schedules, and reactive spending patterns that no one had previously connected.

As the AI began generating forward-looking projections, Priya experienced a profound shift in how financial conversations unfolded, because instead of debating past decisions, leadership discussions centered on future scenarios, evaluating how hiring plans, technology investments, and market expansion would affect tax exposure six, twelve, and twenty-four months ahead. The system flagged upcoming periods where tax liability would spike unless expenses were restructured, prompting proactive adjustments in purchasing schedules and asset acquisitions that smoothed cash flow without slowing growth, demonstrating how predictive insight could reshape decisions long before consequences became unavoidable.

Over time, the AI grew more precise, refining its forecasts as actual outcomes fed back into the models, learning which strategies produced stability and which introduced volatility, gradually transforming tax planning from a once-a-year exercise into an ongoing strategic discipline embedded in everyday decision-making.

What surprised Priya most was how the system changed organizational behavior, because managers began asking better questions, requesting forecasts before committing to major expenditures, and viewing expense decisions through a long-term lens rather than short-term urgency, creating a culture of financial awareness that extended far beyond the finance department.

By the end of the second year, the company closed its books with no surprises, no emergency reallocations, and no reactive tax maneuvers, because every major outcome had already been modeled, discussed, and planned for months in advance, turning what had once been stressful uncertainty into confident execution.

In the third year, during an external audit and strategic review, stakeholders were impressed not only by clean records, but by the company's ability to articulate its future tax position with clarity and confidence, demonstrating a level of financial maturity that increased trust, valuation, and strategic flexibility.

Looking back, Priya realized that the greatest transformation was not technological but psychological, because once the company could see the year before it happened, fear gave way to foresight, reaction gave way to intention, and financial strategy became a tool for leadership rather than a constraint imposed after the fact.

Chapter 10

Building a Permanent Advantage With AI-Driven Tax Systems

The final evolution of AI-powered expense tracking, deductions, and depreciation is not a feature or a workflow, but a permanent structural advantage, because when artificial intelligence is embedded deeply into a business's financial architecture, tax optimization stops being something that requires attention, effort, or specialized knowledge, and instead becomes an automatic outcome of how the business operates every single day.

A permanent advantage is created when systems do not merely execute tasks, but reinforce correct behavior continuously, and AI-driven tax systems do exactly that by ensuring that every transaction, asset purchase, payroll decision, and operational expense is evaluated within a consistent, intelligent framework that aligns compliance, optimization, and long-term strategy without requiring constant intervention from owners, accountants, or advisors.

Unlike traditional tax planning, which depends heavily on human memory, timing, and interpretation, AI systems institutionalize intelligence, capturing knowledge about deductions, depreciation, audit patterns, and regulatory changes in a form that does not disappear when employees leave, advisors change, or business models evolve, ensuring that financial discipline survives growth, turnover, and complexity.

This permanence is especially valuable in a business environment where regulations change frequently, enforcement strategies evolve, and economic conditions shift unexpectedly, because AI systems continuously ingest new data, update classification logic, and adjust optimization strategies in real time, allowing businesses to remain compliant and efficient without disruption or reactive overhauls.

AI-driven tax systems also create compounding benefits, because each year of clean, optimized financial data improves the accuracy of future predictions, strengthens audit defensibility, and enhances strategic planning, meaning that the longer the system operates, the more valuable it becomes, transforming financial history into a strategic asset rather than a static archive.

From an operational standpoint, this permanent advantage frees leadership from tactical concerns, because instead of questioning whether expenses are being tracked correctly or deductions are being missed, decision-makers can focus on growth, innovation, and opportunity, knowing that the financial infrastructure beneath them is intelligently managing risk, compliance, and optimization without constant oversight.

Ultimately, businesses that adopt AI-driven tax systems are not simply reducing their tax bills, they are redefining their relationship with money itself, replacing uncertainty with structure, reaction with foresight, and fragmentation with coherence, creating organizations that retain more capital, scale with confidence, and operate with a level of financial intelligence that becomes increasingly difficult for competitors to replicate over time.

The Quiet Company That Always Won

When Thomas Reed founded his manufacturing analytics firm, he never set out to build the most profitable company in his industry, because his ambition was simpler and, in many ways, more elusive: he wanted to build a business that felt stable, predictable, and resilient, one that could grow without the constant financial stress he had witnessed in other companies rise and fall around him.

In the early years, Thomas focused on products, customers, and talent, while handling finances competently but conventionally, relying on accountants, periodic reviews, and end-of-year tax planning, believing that stability would naturally emerge as the company matured, yet despite steady revenue growth, financial uncertainty lingered, resurfacing every tax season in the form of unexpected liabilities and reactive decisions.

The shift came gradually, not through a dramatic crisis, but through a realization that stability could not be achieved through effort alone, because no matter how disciplined his team was, human systems could not match the consistency required to manage thousands of transactions, assets, and regulatory rules over many years without drift, error, or fatigue.

After implementing an AI-driven tax and expense intelligence system, Thomas noticed something subtle but profound happening beneath the surface of the business, because while daily operations looked unchanged, the financial layer of the company began to behave differently, capturing expenses automatically, optimizing deductions continuously, and aligning depreciation schedules with long-term growth rather than short-term convenience.

In the first year, the impact was modest but noticeable, fewer surprises, cleaner reports, and smoother cash flow, but it was in the second and third years that the true power of permanence emerged, as each tax cycle reinforced the next building a coherent financial narrative that grew stronger clearer, and more defensible with time. As competitors expanded aggressively, often chasing growth without structure, Thomas's company expanded deliberately, guided by predictive insights that showed how new investments would affect taxes, cash flow, and profitability years into the future, allowing leadership to choose opportunities that aligned with long-term stability rather than short-term hype.

By the fourth year, audits became routine formalities rather than sources of anxiety, because the company's records told a consistent story of disciplined spending, intentional investment, and continuous optimization, leaving little room for doubt or dispute, and reinforcing trust among regulators, partners, and investors alike.

What distinguished Thomas's company most was not its margins or revenue growth alone, but its predictability, because forecasts matched outcomes with uncanny accuracy, allowing the business to plan expansions, acquisitions, and hiring with confidence, while competitors remained reactive, adjusting strategy after financial surprises forced their hand.

In the fifth and sixth years, this predictability translated into opportunity, as investors valued the company higher than peers with similar revenue, recognizing that its financial architecture reduced risk and increased long-term reliability, turning what had once been invisible discipline into tangible strategic leverage. By the seventh year, Thomas realized that the company had quietly built something rare, a system that did not rely on constant vigilance, heroics, or last-minute fixes, but instead reinforced good decisions automatically, year after year, transaction by transaction, making financial intelligence a permanent feature rather than a temporary effort.

Looking back, Thomas understood that the company always won not because it was more aggressive or more ambitious, but because it was structurally smarter, having embedded intelligence into its foundation in a way that compounded quietly over time, proving that the most powerful advantages in business are often the ones that work silently, consistently, and long after you stop paying attention to them.

Final Thoughts

The End of Manual Taxes and the Beginning of Intelligent Business Finance

Artificial intelligence has quietly ended an era in business finance, the era where tax efficiency depended on memory, manual processes, delayed reviews, and fragmented systems that could never fully reflect how modern businesses actually operate, and what this book has shown, chapter by chapter, is that AI does not merely improve expense tracking, deductions, or depreciation, but fundamentally changes the relationship between a business and its money by embedding intelligence directly into every financial decision, transaction, and system.

Throughout this book, one truth has become increasingly clear: most businesses do not fail to optimize taxes because they lack discipline or intent, but because the complexity of modern operations exceeds human capacity to track, classify, and strategize consistently over time, and AI resolves this mismatch by replacing limitation with structure, uncertainty with prediction, and reactivity with design, allowing businesses of any size to operate with the financial sophistication once reserved only for large corporations with elite advisory teams. AI-powered expense tracking turns everyday spending into a continuous source of insight, capturing deductions humans miss, applying depreciation with mathematical precision, and maintaining audit-ready records automatically, while predictive intelligence allows businesses to see tax outcomes before they happen, aligning spending, investment, and growth decisions with long-term financial objectives rather than short-term urgency.

Perhaps most importantly, AI creates permanence, because financial intelligence no longer disappears when personnel changes, advisors rotate, or business models evolve, but instead becomes institutionalized within systems that learn, adapt, and improve year after year, compounding advantages quietly in the background while leadership focuses on innovation, customers, and growth.

What this means for the future of business is profound, because companies that adopt AI-driven tax systems are not merely reducing their tax bills, they are building resilient financial architectures that scale without chaos, comply without fear, and optimize without constant effort, creating organizations that retain more capital, attract higher valuations, and operate with confidence in an increasingly complex regulatory and economic environment. As you close this book, the question is no longer whether AI will transform business taxation, because that transformation is already underway, but whether your business will continue to rely on outdated, reactive methods, or step into a future where intelligence is embedded, optimization is automatic, and financial clarity becomes a permanent competitive advantage rather than a recurring struggle.

The era of manual tax management is ending, and the era of intelligent, self-optimizing business finance has already begun, and the businesses that embrace it now will quietly outperform those that do not for years to come.

www.ingramcontent.com/pod-product-compliance
Ingram Content Group UK Ltd.
Pitfield, Milton Keynes, MK11 3LW, UK
UKHW020155290926
15471UKWH00005B/883

9 798295 593291